Whatever happened to the dinosaurs?

W9-DHS-821

Written and illustrated by Bernard Most

A TRUMPET CLUB SPECIAL EDITION

Whatever happened to the dinosaurs?

Published by The Trumpet Club
666 Fifth Avenue, New York, New York 10103

Copyright © 1984 by Bernard Most

ISBN 0-440-84745-1

This edition published by arrangement with
Harcourt Brace Jovanovich, Inc.
Printed in the United States of America
November 1991

10 9 8 7 6 5 4 3 2 1
UPC

To every child (or grown-up)
who ever wondered about the dinosaurs.

We love to visit the library and read
all about the dinosaurs.
   But where did all the dinosaurs go?
   They were so big and there were
so many of them.
   Why did they disappear?
   Nobody knows. Even scientists
are not sure.
   The more we read about them,
the more we wonder:

   Whatever happened to the dinosaurs?

Did all the dinosaurs go
to another planet?
    Maybe they're on
Jupiter or Mars.

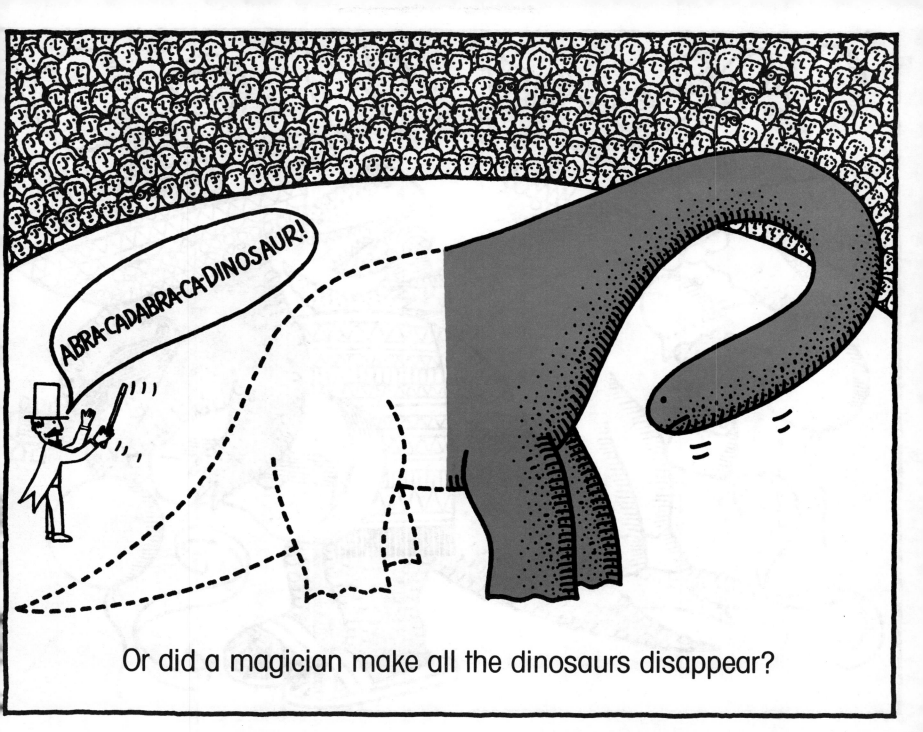

Or did a magician make all the dinosaurs disappear?

Maybe the dinosaurs are wearing disguises
and we just don't recognize them.

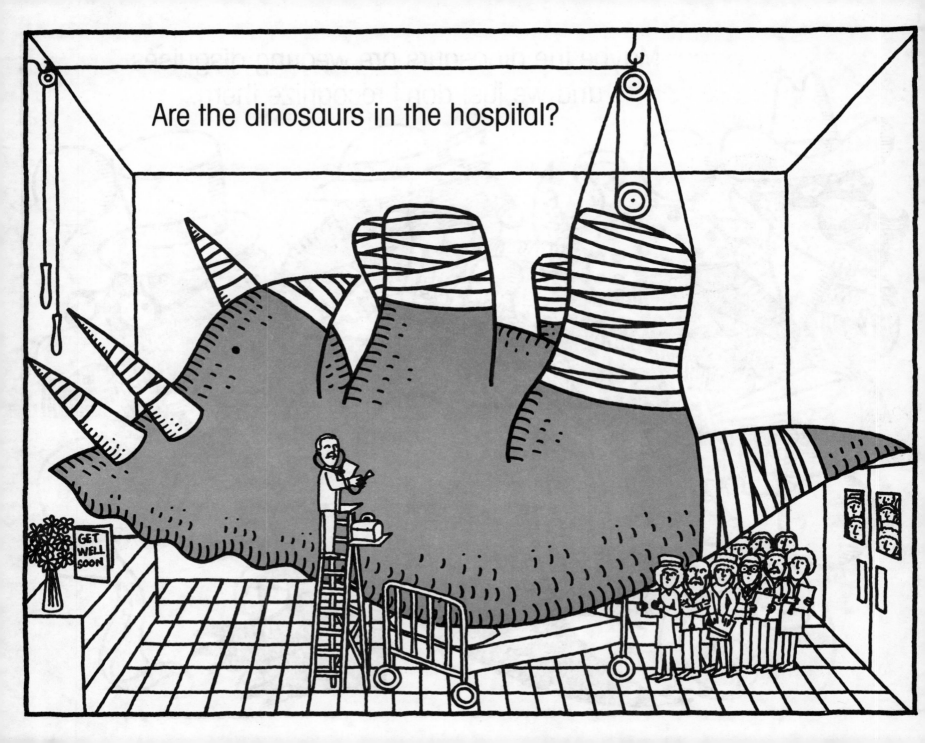

Or are they in jail?

Maybe the dinosaurs are lost
in the middle of the jungle.

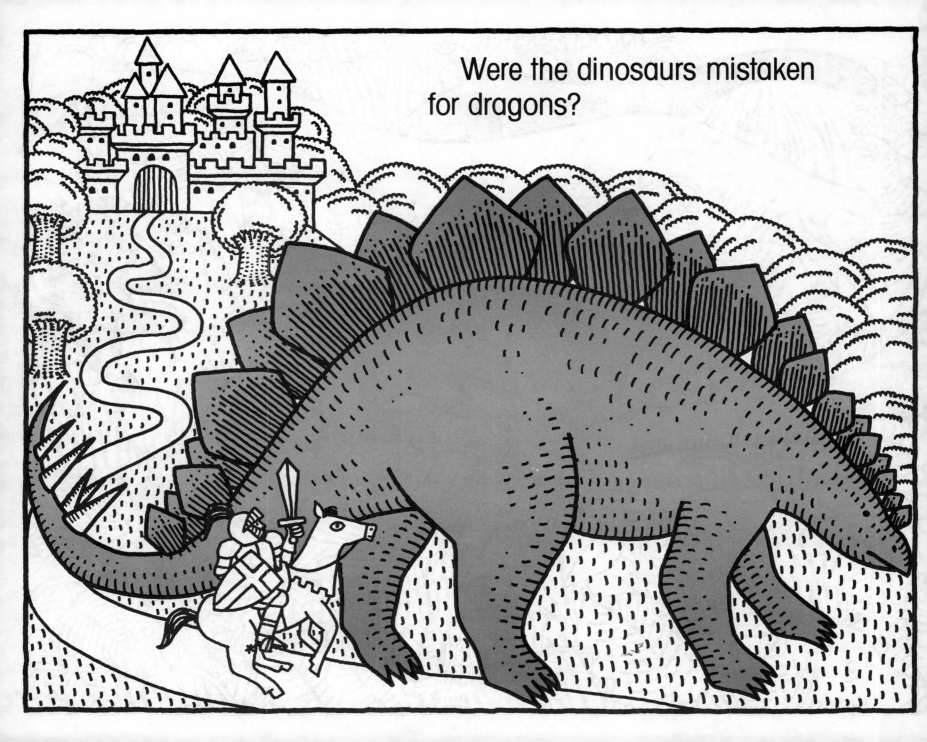

Were the dinosaurs mistaken for dragons?

Or did pirates steal them away?

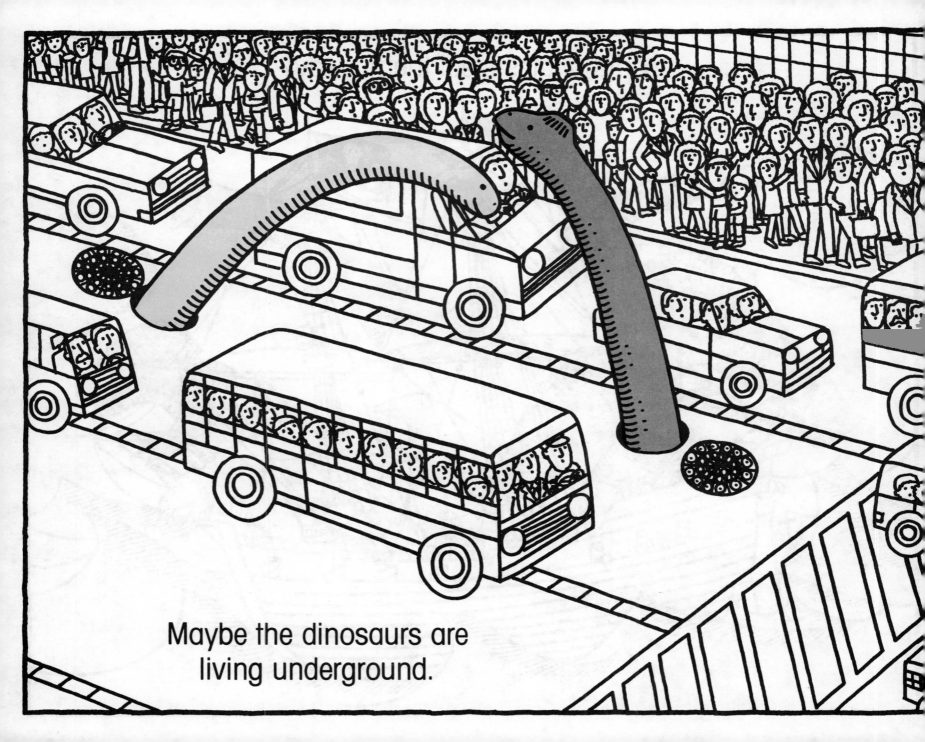

Maybe the dinosaurs are
living underground.

Did all the dinosaurs go on vacation?

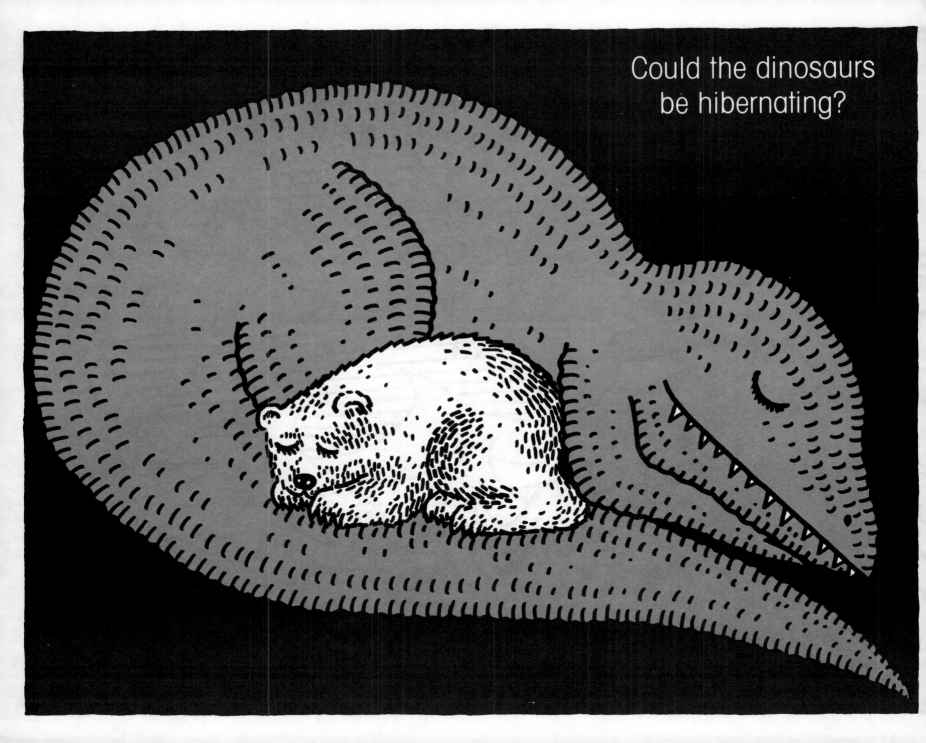

Could the dinosaurs
be hibernating?

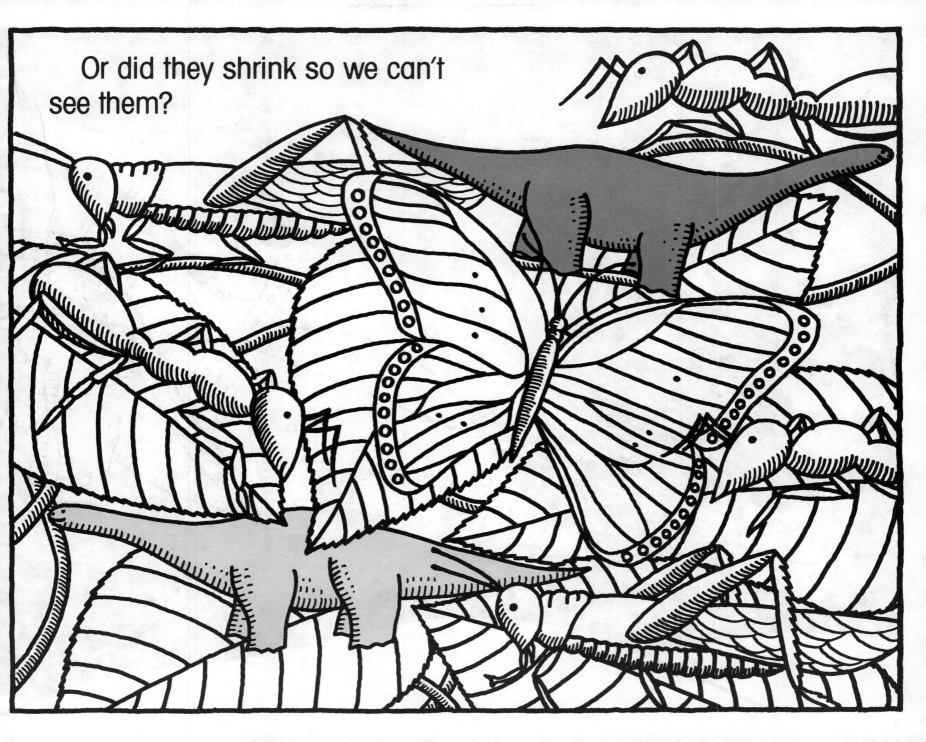

Or did they shrink so we can't see them?

Maybe the dinosaurs are
at the North Pole.

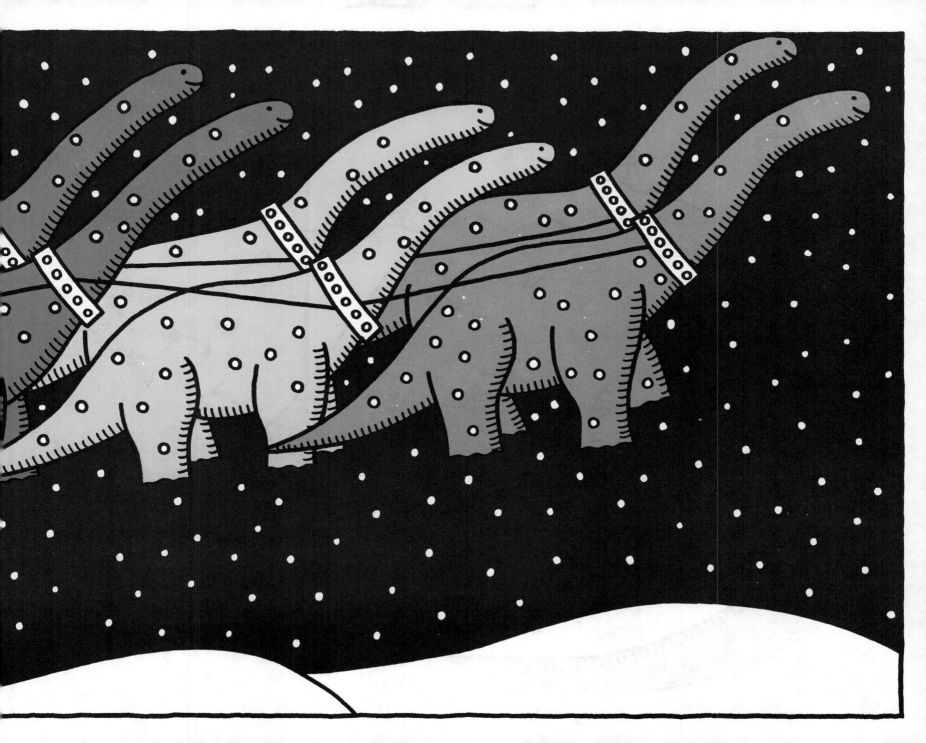

Are the dinosaurs underwater?

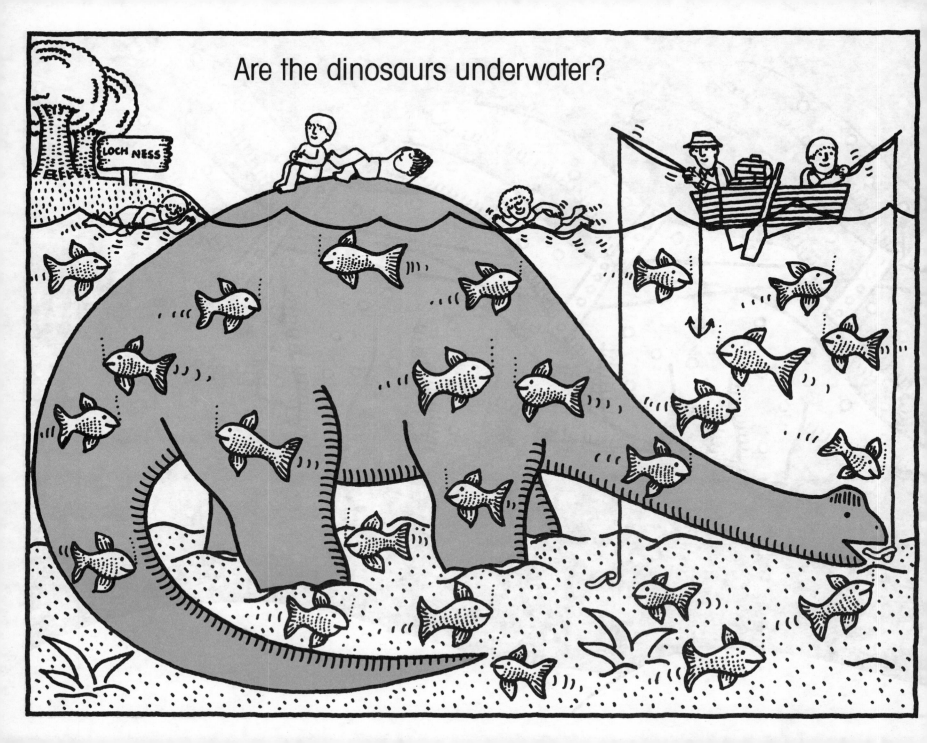

Are the dinosaurs playing hide-and-seek?

Maybe some day somebody will discover whatever happened to the dinosaurs.

Whatever happened to the Allosaurus,
the Brachiosaurus, the Camptosaurus,
the Ceratosaurus, the Cetiosaurus,
the Coelophysis, the Corythosaurus,
the Dimetrodon, the Diplodocus,
the Hypselosaurus, the Iguanodon,
the Megalosaurus, the Monoclonius,
the Ornithomimus, the Parasaurolophus,
the Plateosaurus, the Plesiosaurus,
the Protoceratops, the Scelidosaurus,
the Stegosaurus, the Trachodon,
the Triceratops, and the Tyrannosaurus?

Do you know?